LEARNING TO LOVE

TEN STEPS TO EMPOWERED (SELF) LOVE AND (INNER) PEACE

By Rodney J. Ferris

© November 1, 2010

LCCN 2010937553

ISBN 978-0-615-40312-0

DEDICATION

This book is dedicated to spiritual seekers on their way home and to humanity, which seems to have lost its way. Further, it is dedicated to the billions of our brothers and sisters who have been wiped out prematurely since the beginning of our time on this planet by natural and unnatural catastrophes. Their collective appreciation of and yearning for love is our most profound legacy.

Tragically, their dreams of love have become like sand particles shining brilliantly in the sun and spread over all the earth. Our sacred blessing is to give sanctuary to their being and aspire to manifest what they so longingly sought, remembering what they lost as we realize for them the love that it is our potential to reawaken. It is their collective love and that of the Supreme Power in the universe that lives in us now, if we can only sense, feel, touch and "see" to appreciate and manifest it.

CONTENTS

Acknowledgments

Acknowledging all the contributors to this book is a practical impossibility, for it is the product of all I have learned in my seventy-seven years on the planet; furthermore, you would be bored to tears if I even tried!

This book is intended as a prequel to my book, **Holy Love,** which is a workbook that elaborates and expands on what you are about to read, so if your hunger persists after our short sojourn together, you may want to consider what it can offer to you.

Learning to Love presents an invitation to change the way you live your life. It may be "over the top" for you at this stage, but your having picked it up for perusal may suggest more than a casual interest in discovering something that may make a profound difference to you, sooner or later.

I want to incorporate in the acknowledgments for this book all of the influences I recognized in **Holy Love**. In addition to those, there are some special people I want to mention here who have been helpful to me in designing and producing this prequel.

As I was focused on making **Holy Love** useful, I talked to people, established a Web site and actively sought answers to the distribution riddle I had produced. I was led to Bill Densmore, a director of the **Center for Non-Violent Solutions** in Worcester, Massachusetts. He encouraged me to write up my ideas about love.

So challenged, I wrote a draft that seemed almost complete until Rich Nobile, a neighbor in our condo community, invited me to make a presentation to the community on **The Mysteries of Prehistory**. So I took a respite from writing the draft of **Learning to Love** and researched instead what I could find on prehistory. After making the presentation six months later, I decided to get back to my book draft and realized that I now had a new and significant perspective that became its first chapter.

I circulated a succession of drafts to special friends and asked for advice. I am very grateful for the following readers who gave me valuable insight and suggestions: Rev. Paul Kennedy; Rev. Barbara Ward; Jackie Morelewicz; Tammy Butler; Louise Virgin; Wendy Greeney; my son Dakin Ferris and his business partner, Evan Margolin; Mary Frost; and Lori Carlson-Hijuelos.

Herstory[1]

Once upon a time she and he were in a dream, a dream they shared in almost all respects. It was a dream of how life could be: could be warm, could be peaceful, could be together as one, could be comfortable, could be as we wish, could be as we dream... This dream was one of loving and loyal presence in sacred space. There was little functional choice in this life for individuals.

As they turned toward each other in the early dawn, realizing their sensuous proximity as well as their shared dreaming, they touched gently, knowing through that touch that they were a beautiful essence called life, on a mysterious, living planet that pursued a transcendent trajectory into an unknown future.

Further, they knew they were immersed in a living consciousness, that the universe, of which they were a significant part, was where everything was interconnected in a web-like pattern of exquisite beauty and mystery. In this consciousness they knew they were not alone, that they

---

[1] We already know his-tory! Since **Learning to Love** requires stimulating the right side of the brain, creating an intuitive awareness, I begin this book with a symbolic stimulus that is feminine in orientation. In addition, since history has typically been presented by left-brained analysts, presumably male, isn't it about time to recognize the legitimacy of an alternative perspective, albeit from a right-brained male who lives in both sides?

1

were immersed in a divine design that was more grand and more esoteric than their imaginations could conceive of.[2]

One characteristic of this time was a way of being that involved a **sacred seeing** that was different from the way we see today. It involved becoming immersed in what was to be seen so that the effect on the seer was a sensory, visceral essence within life. There was a sense of unity with the object seen, as though both seer and the object seen knew each other intimately; they were so close as to be inseparable. Love was made real by this intimacy with everybody, everything and beyond everything, a constant reminder of its power and beauty. Being in this loving reality made their touching deeply felt, so that the effect was almost constantly in the realm of joy.

As consciousness developed in time they found others who shared their same feelings of unity with life, of spiritual wholeness, of natural goodness. They worked hard together in order to create more understanding, more comfort, more labor-saving innovations, more beauty and more spiritual deepening.

Beauty for them included sophisticated and intuitive levels of symmetry and form. They developed the beauty and deepest meanings of what we know today as spirituality and numerology, utilizing these concepts in

---

[2] Native American and worldwide cultures have handed down a similar sense of consciousness from herstory. It is our common legacy.

architectural and other kinds of design. Much of this knowing felt deeply intuitive, unified and spiritual.

They knew from a deep place within that they were unique in the universe. Taking steps to explore their planet, they mapped the stars above, discovering the rhythms of the moon, the planets, the path of their home planet, and many of the mysteries of existence. Their way was to see the blessing and beneficence inherent in all they discovered.

As time went on and many thousands of generations passed, disturbances to their idyllic journey created anxiety and unexpected death and chaos for multitudes. The planet seemed to have a way of being that, although benign in many respects, occasionally asserted an unusually disruptive influence on life. They knew that they were part of a dynamic aliveness only part of which they could understand and predict. They lived in ambient uncertainty, making the dependable rhythms of life a blessing that elicited spontaneous gratitude.

Responding to uncertainty, they sought to discover what caused these periodic disruptions by erecting megalithic structures like pyramids and holy places like London, Jerusalem, Stonehenge, Tiahuanaco, Easter Island and Machu Picchu (to name only a few) in a regular pattern around their world. In designing these megaliths they incorporated the elegance of their intuitive intelligence.

In so doing they sought to measure how the poles of the earth shifted from time to time and by how much. Incorporated in this exploration was the realization that the crust of the earth could suddenly shift in one piece, as well as more slowly in separate tectonic pieces.[3]

Knowing how periodic earth crust shifts could send tidal waves over much of the earth's surface, how earthquakes could destroy, how the fabric of life could be altered, and in the spirit of feeling a great joy in loving life, they sought to communicate their knowledge in a form that would allow survivors of these cataclysms to one day discover what they had spent so much effort learning, in case their progeny couldn't live to do it directly. The Pyramids and Sphinx in Egypt, the construction mechanics of which have so far eluded our ability to understand, attest to their craft and wisdom.[4]

Furthermore, out of experience in living and as they proliferated, they eventually discovered that they had fundamental choice. The discovery of this sense of choice was revelatory, since for millennia life was communal and communication was often telepathic. Generally, almost everyone acted as one being, making the building of civilization a unified way of feeling and being, in which almost all felt unity of purpose.

---

[3] See Rand & Rose Flem-Ath: **When the Sky Fell**

[4] See Colin Wilson: **Atlantis & The Kingdom of the Neanderthals**; Malkowski: **Before the Pharaohs**

Choice evolved as another way of being, which took a long time to become digestible, as it broke apart at times the unified way of being. Reconciling this split became in time a spiritual art form, still in the process of creation as I write.

Out of the initial way of synchronous harmony with nature and the spirit of the universe, the birth of choice created at least two polar views for the way of being. One carried on the spirit of harmony, reconciliation and peace, all evolved from love; the other, forged out of recognition of inherent threat by the apparent instability of the earth and of fellow humans motivated by fear and anxiety, a way of being characterized by independence, competition, conquest, and greed, all evolved from fear and a perceived need for self-preservation, and psychological neediness.

In 9,600 BCE it happened as they had forecast. Almost everyone and almost everything was destroyed or encased in ice, repeating the human tragedy that occurred about every forty-one thousand years. The North Pole shifted from Hudson's Bay to its present location as the two American continents shifted two thousand miles south and the temperate zone of Antarctica, known as Atlantis, moved into the south polar region and became encased under thousands of feet of ice.

In time, those who survived the major earth crust shift were further harassed by meteors that struck the planet, as well as by earthquakes and volcanic eruptions. The comparative few who survived, not being as wise or as accomplished as their predecessors, didn't appreciate what they had inherited.

But they did retain enough knowledge to simultaneously initiate the production of agricultural products in the highlands of the remaining temperate regions of the world. They also kept alive as best they could the memories of their past through what we today call myth.

Then, sometime in the period around 1,250 BCE, rational thought began to arise as a predominant way of being. Inheriting some of the legacy from our prehistory, math and science became progressively established and worshipped by the newest and most daring of the cultures that arose out of choice.

This new way of left-brained thinking and being came along to produce the history we have come to know. Whereas right-brain thinking based on intuition and holistic views of the universe had dominated in the prior civilization(s), now left-brain rational thinking began to dominate, as people found benefit in taking things apart and trying to discern what laws of nature were inherent. As this left-brained milieu seemed more practical and productive, it gained adherents who began to ignore the more right-brained aspects of their inheritance.

Thus, the old nature-based spirituality, such as today's Wicca and other indigenous religious remnants, was almost wiped out.   In the left-brained dominated culture in the Western and Middle-Eastern nations, love was remembered and presented as the answer without telling people how to do it and without embodying it, in a kind of lip-service to a distant memory. This happened because our ancestors were unaware that they were losing touch with an important aspect of their prehistory. In a right-brain world there was no need to teach how to love because that was the only way of being!

Today we live in a world where precious few religious leaders deny the power of love, but where the loss of right-brained thinking/feeling is unrecognized as such, which is one reason for the creation of this book. We seem to have collectively lost the ability to manifest love consciously in daily life, primarily, I would argue, because our left-brained way of being cannot "see" what love is all about. "Seeing" the collective legacy of love mentioned in the dedication to this book is significant, and it can only be appreciated through your right brain.

Furthermore, Eastern religions based on much more ancient codes emphasize seeking spirituality within. These religions tend to have more in common with ancient, right-brained traditions than in the West, where the alternative has often emphasized authoritarian liturgy and perhaps inadvertently established a culture of spiritual co-dependency. An exception is The Society of Friends, the Quakers.

Inherent in the logic of rationality operating in the context of pervasive fear and greed, warfare has become entrenched as a way of life, leading to discoveries of new ways of killing people in greater and greater numbers. Financiers have found ways to steal the wealth of nations by fomenting endless war.

The value of love as a way of being was slowly usurped by a focus on greed, killing and self-centered myopia, to the horror and lamentation of more holistic minorities. Even the aristocratic potentates of organized religion have become immunized from substantive objection to the outrage. Tears shed throughout herstory have been insufficient to influence or ameliorate official policy. The absence of compassion for the billions of victims of genocide is appalling.

What's more, the invention of the Internet for high-speed world-wide communication and the need to make owners wealthy by farming out productive labor from the United States to the cheapest world bidder, stealthily combined to assist in taking over once-remote societies from an antiquity geared mostly to love. An esoteric, unnoticed war of the sacred versus the profane began to consume the spiritual quest of mankind.

The world today is imploding from a modern form of barbarism that sees love and compassion as wasted forms of ineffectualness. The result is that we cannot see the disease that envelops us all, especially as we race to catch the gravy train.

And thus, we arrive at today, where financiers are still busily destroying what's left of the earth. Beauty has been bulldozed and shoveled into oblivion, while the people have become internally lost in the nihilism and distractions of modern life. And democratic government has been corrupted by corporate largesse with Supreme Court blessing, so that laws are being purchased in spite of the people rather than created for their benefit.

Democracy is in a struggle for survival, as is the earth, poisoned by the rampant, obscene and irresponsible pursuit of money and power. For example, dumping waste into the sea and into the air, or hiding it underground are the irresponsible methods of the profane.

Do we have to wait for our children to die from the poisons before we wake up? Our sacred planet is not a garbage dump, but that's how we're treating it. It is so profoundly saddening and outrageous.

And so we are left with a critical question: Is love lost? Dead? Gone forever? Is the sacred way of seeing through utilization of the right side of our brains so dim a memory that our access into being is forever emasculated?

Or can it become resurgent? Can the phoenix of love ever arise from the ashes? The answer may determine the fate of the planet, not to mention what's left of civilization.

There is some hope, however. Richard Louv's book, **Last Child in the Woods,** has illuminated the loss of contact with nature that has consumed our society. When he and I grew up, we lived close to and in the woods, playing in intimate contact with nature. Too many of today's children are being denied that kind of experience by having their intimate contact restricted to video games, PlayStations, and TV cartoons. In too many cases Wii games have replaced more natural ones. Marvelous as these inventions are, they rob our children of intimacy with nature, which is one key to right-brained appreciation of real life. Educators and parents, through Louv's book and others, are responding with changes. Will they be sufficient? Are enough people caring that this issue is addressed? Do they have any idea how important it is?

Let's now leave herstory and seek an experiential answer to this gargantuan struggle, journeying into our sacred selves with sacred seeing, and in so doing remind ourselves of our unique heritage. Open to the possibility of personal transformation as you read.

Preface

Learning to Love: This may seem like an odd subject for a book! You may be saying: "But love is so easy! Why do I need to read about something I already know about? Love seems like it's the way life is for me. Is there really something I don't know about love that would make me pick up this book and read it? Besides, what was lost from life so long ago in herstory seems too remote and irrelevant to me. I feel more like a good novel instead! And, anyway, it's time to cook dinner..."

Or you may be saying, "This looks like sissy stuff. I wouldn't be caught dead reading it! I feel more like a novel about my favorite sports heroes. Maybe I don't want any book right now—books are not energetic enough for me. Come-on, let's go get a beer and watch the ballgame."

Why might people have these or similar reactions? I believe a case can be made that love is the most underrated and necessary commodity on the planet right now. Once upon a time in herstory, love united civilization into creative, sacred living. If love is the key to peace, why isn't love our first priority today? Why not read about the most important subject on the planet right now? I hope to solve the mystery for you of why love may seem so irrelevant Otherwise you may never know what you missed! Curious? Read on for some more thoughts on this.

11

If we stop to reflect a moment, we may begin to wonder whether something is missing from our approach to living, especially as we step off the treadmill of life as we know it and/or wake up sober after a night of trying to forget. What am I really trying to forget? Why? Is it the sense of what sacred seeing sought?

Is peace possible through love? Can you imagine the energy of love permeating the life of everyone on the planet, forgetting for the moment the practical issue of achieving this state? If the pursuit of self-serving power and greed became subordinated and perhaps eliminated by the value and energy of love, what would the difference be? Would war then be possible? Would violence then be possible? Would racism then be possible? Would discrimination then be possible?

Isn't the truth that a love that permeated life on the planet would bring peace?

Is this not desirable?

So what we need to talk about is the process for achieving such a state!

There may be times when we need to step back from life, globally and personally, and ponder what it's all about. Is this one of them? Read on!

"Only one life
That soon will pass;
Only what's done
With love will last."
Anonymous[5]

Step 1: Life: What's It All About Anyway?

It's hard to imagine a tougher question, given the turmoil on the planet. At one extreme there is the violence of war, murder, rape and pillage; at another there is a shortage of food, whether healthy or poisoned; at another, entire nations of peoples are facing extinction due to rising sea levels, loss of ice, escalating storms or rapidly advancing regions of drought; at another, even within the USA, there is traffic in human beings for sexual exploitation; and at another there are corrupt governments, living off other people like you and me, and perpetrating genocide, as in Vietnam, Darfur, Rwanda, Iraq, Iran, the Congo, and Afghanistan.

These extremes are perhaps fringe considerations, given where you are likely to be when you read this, but I have to assume, that with global communications at the speed of light, you haven't missed all the news. What you may have missed is a sense of horror over what collectively we have perpetrated. Or are there no tears left with which

---

[5] Many years ago, this was quoted as a mantelpiece inscription from an old house in England; it inspired my journey then and still does.

to cry? Are you among those who are in denial about what is happening? Do you care?

Most Americans literally live in the culture of our minds in the Wild West with unholstered six-guns at the ready. We know that our history, as depicted in any U.S. history book and in late-night movies, is one of war, killing and violence. (I grew up memorizing the dates of wars and recalling what always irresolvable causes produced the next war. There was little reference to peace except as the space and time between conflicts. There was certainly no reverence for peace, except in the world of poets.)

I would argue that we are all suffering from the PTSD (Post Traumatic Stress Disorder) of generations of war, murder, killing, and violence, suffused within our culture so that we don't recognize it any more as a significant part of our condition. Anyone familiar with the product of war knows PTSD intimately: It is a condition extremely difficult to heal. Our national efforts at healing, such as they are, seem to be dysfunctional at best; we don't even recognize that we all need healing from our outrageous and inglorious past. Our politicians and the media make special efforts to "spin" history so that we can live in comfortable denial.

Thus, our children are currently condemned to absorb, directly and indirectly, that violence and killing are the norm, not the sicknesses they really are. Bullies in the schoolyard are endemic; mental and physical abuse of those with differences is systemic. And then we wonder why so many of our "innocent" children grow up to become killers and abusers. Don't we become what we live? Why isn't this seen as obvious?

But war, murder and violence are symptoms of a larger trauma: the impact of technological civilization on humans who were created to live much closer to nature and the sacred, as herstory tells us. What we experience today in life is what a left-brained culture, cut off from right-brained sensitivity, has produced.

Could individuals in our civilization today be described as being somewhat estranged or cut off from each other and from reality? Could our general psychological state be described as dissociated—i.e., like having a split personality where part of us is no longer present?

I believe that our collective, addiction-prone and dissociative response to life has forced us into a social pathology that is not only difficult to comprehend and understand but, even when recognized, to deal with. The need to heal this woundedness is pervasive. If we must look at violence with the objective of attaining peace, we must begin by looking at the trauma integral to our corner of civilization.

In addition, it is worth noting that TV violence and video games are ubiquitous, teaching our children that a life is worthless and, if someone is in your way, then you kill him. Even walking around with headphones or earpieces, or cell phones and iPhones, Blackberries, etc., all serve to separate us from natural sounds and beauty in our environment. That separation typically creates anxiety and disconnection from nature by substituting connection through man-made technology. If we live so that major time is spent so removed, then the resultant anxiety may eventually create anger that can lead to or exacerbate tendencies toward violence. We need community and closeness to nature, not isolation or diversion. That we don't realize this is happening to us is first-magnitude tragedy.

Our children thus have to deal with an insecure and disconnected environment that provides little opportunity to gain a wholesome sense of themselves. Since so many adults in our culture are sick with this cultural disease, there are precious few models from which our children can draw healing. That itself is **pathetic**.

Thus, peace is the exception in our culture, not the rule. We are trained to "fight the good fight," to win at all costs, to be the "fittest" to survive, etc. We teach or condone hatred of differences; we model dysfunction from the highest officials in our land to the lowest functionaries. The answer seems to be violence, no matter what the provocation.

Peace is somewhere elusive, lost among the mountains and the prairies, lost in the deserts, lost in the night, lost in the fog, lost along the seashores, lost in the silence of the forests. It's just MIA. But where people must live in close proximity, peace seems to be too often absent: It doesn't seem to be on anyone's radar screen!

So how do you, in average circumstances, make a choice about how to live your life? Fishing for the response, another question is to ask what your spirit is called to do right now.

Is life about survival? Is it about making sure you've got enough of life's shelter and food to "make it?" Is it about greed—I've got to accumulate enough wealth to take care of me and mine and to hell with everyone else? Or is it about "doing my job," "keeping my nose to the grindstone," or some other slogan to hide behind, hoping the world's problems don't impact me in some unfortunate way?

Other good questions to ask are: What's most important in my life? Where does sacred seeing fit in?

There are many choices, many more than can be enumerated here. To reduce these questions to something more workable, perhaps there is a parameter of relative measurement that can help sort out the puzzle: Am I going to add to life's problems (whether for me or for others), or am I part of the solution, no matter how effective, no matter how insignificant? Is my life more about helping myself and others live a better life, or is it just about me and what I can get out of it? Or is it about not making a choice at all but living each day as it comes and doing the best I can to

17

get by, allowing the tides, winds and other circumstances to bend me to chance encounters or activities?

Does choosing to be part of the problem mean that you have been suckered into thinking less of yourself than you are worth, of thinking you have no redemptive future, or that you are not worthy of being as good as you can be? If this is part of your burden, perhaps you need to examine why you feel that way and re-choose.

To be part of the solution requires another perspective. It means making a contribution, no matter how seemingly insignificant, to helping ease the pain and chaos that exists on the planet right now.

If this is your choice and commitment, then love must enter the milieu in which you find yourself. To focus on one of the world's problems with the objective of trying to help, where that help is easing someone's pain, then the effort you apply must involve love at some level. The question is: at what level?

Wouldn't it then help you in your quest to have a better sense of what love is all about? Would sacred seeing help you in this quest?

I wonder if the Christian Church has done Christians an injustice by emphasizing that we only need to love others. There is a natural fear among ecclesiastical leaders of narcissism, that trap of overindulgent self-love. Unfortunately, their reluctance to allow the engagement of healthy self-love may have contributed to the lethargy that surrounds the subject. Is this perhaps why pursuing an examination of love is such a turn-off?

Do you really know what love is all about? Perhaps you need to be a little more certain of the answer! Perhaps it is worth some reflection on love in order to choose a life that makes a difference.

If you are considering reading a book like this one, and the topic may seem too removed from everyday needs to inspire your getting into it, what is in the way? Given the state of the world, it would be easy to become discouraged or depressed. Instant multi-media communication certainly makes it difficult to ignore the ravages of mankind and nature.

Of course, another option is to drug yourself so as to be out of touch with and thereby escape all of this. But then you have to find a way to purchase those drugs, which eventually leads down a slippery slope to dissolution, decay and death. There must be a better way!

There is a better way. If the world needs love and you are a vital part of that world, why wouldn't you want to know more about what you might want to do differently? Or how you want to BE differently? Being "too busy" seems like a questionable answer to this inquiry, if that's how you feel. An alternative right now is to continue reading!

STEP 2: Love Elaborated[6]

This step calls you to consider what love really is. I encourage you to reflect on this and take in more than the words I'm using to probe the meaning of love. You might consider closing your eyes at some point in the following, just to sense what your subconscious mind does with this space.

The closest the *Merriam-Webster Dictionary* comes to the definition of the love I speak of is to define it as "unselfish loyal and benevolent concern for others." (Notice the absence of the word "self:" the definition should be "concern for <u>self</u> and others." Do I discern a dysfunctional bias here?) But I would go deeper and add: it is a means to an end, a consciously-chosen commitment to act in a certain way that flows from a deep well of spiritual wholeness (and holiness) that allows us to see ourselves and others as one. It accepts unconditionally the self and others as they are, regardless of their actions, behaviors, skin color, sex, marital preferences or anything else.

Thus, the love I refer to is more a force than an end-state; it is a dynamic of Grace that is in tune with the God-force in the universe, a presence that is all around and within us. It is a feeling of caring or deep respect for yourself and others, of valuing and believing, and of helping to achieve the best of which everyone is capable. It

---

[6] Mostly quoted from **Holy Love**.

often translates into finding a sense of purpose, fulfillment and fun in life, sensing the beauty in all that surrounds you and that you are. To live in love is the elixir of life.

Have you ever stopped to consider the beauty that surrounds us in nature? Why are flowers so beautiful? How did the night sky come to have a moon, so many stars and other features such as the northern lights? How is it that we are human beings? What force has created all the varieties of creatures that share space with us on the planet? How did water come to be formed? Soil? The mountains? What makes everything want to turn green? What makes plants and animals grow? Why are ecosystems self-preserving? All of these questions can only be answered as mystery. I call this mystery: God-force, or just plain God.

Love is that power of the God-force that creates beneficence; it empowers life; it is all that matters. Love is God's energy, manifested in the beauty referred to above. When we love, we invoke the sublime power of God's grace. To learn to love is to open your heart to allow God's loving energy to flow through you. There is no greater power in life than that of God's love. Jesus and other holy masters knew this. The priest, Pierre Teilhard de Chardin, spoke of our finally re-discovering this power as the cleansing fire that would enliven and re-ignite our souls.

It is clear to me that love is what our world needs to evoke in every realm of our existence: our planetary and social ecology, our economics, our politics, our thinking, our spiritual work, our conversations, our relationships, etc.

There is no end to love's beneficial potential and no greater need.

Exploring the application of love is the most powerful calling of the planet right now. Geographic exploration is dying as a calling. No longer "go west young man," or take a space journey to the moon, it is: Go inside to explore love, find yourself in God and apply what you come to know to the needs of a planet that so desperately needs you. Should this be your choice, many blessings. The world awaits you with eagerness.

If you haven't stopped in this STEP to close your eyes and reflect on the meaning of love, do it now!

(This space and others in the text are a message to your subconscious to allow reflection and meditation.)

STEP 3: Love is More Than You Think

I find it interesting, and somewhat amusing, to discover that many people think they know what love means and how to "do" it. Many surely do, but are too many others just kidding themselves?

We use the word, love, so flippantly in poetry, song and everyday talk that no one I've ever heard has even asked: "Well, how do I go about learning to love?" It's as though an answer is unnecessary, not a topic of serious inquiry, and not a subject worth spending time on. Even the Christian Bible offers no instruction on how to become loving, unless some of the poetry in the Song of Solomon fulfills that need. Even there, however, the most we get is an allusion to what love is all about.

What the Christian establishment seems to have missed is the subtlety of Jesus's message. His life was lived *inside of love* as a way of being. The stories in the New Testament tell of his loving work and how powerful and necessary His love was. He taught the importance of love through parables, teaching stories. Unfortunately, none of his (left-brained) disciples with the exception of (right-brained) Mary Magdalen[7], understood being inside of love. To Jesus living love was a way of being in life; so he felt no necessity to teach people how to transform themselves so as to live inside of love. Apparently, he felt that teaching

---

[7] See **Gospel of Mary** by Elaine Pagels

23

parables and his personal living example would be sufficient.

It seems that too many authors, as well as the entire Christian teaching establishment, feel that how to love is so obvious as not to require instruction or a disciplined approach. It seems as though everyone is in agreement that love doesn't need to be defined or learned, that you just need to DO it! The presumed point is to encourage love, but how are we supposed to go about that, really? What do we need to do? How do we need to be? What's it all about? What's the nature of the training we need?

As I search the texts of religious literature and other tomes of truth, I find very little that suggests anyone other than poets and philosophers has ever taken the topic seriously. Why? If love is the way to peace in the world, and peace is so needed, why aren't more people interested in finding out something about it?

And if the world's religions have been aware for millennia that love is the answer to the world's needs, why is it that we have so failed at being loving? How is it that we are still killing each other? Why isn't there a firestorm of protest, or at least concern? How can we hold love as an ideal while living with fear? Isn't there something wrong with this picture?

Are our collective expectations so jaded that we have given up before we've even begun?

I wonder if it has to do with the esoteric nature of heart energy and the way that energy comes to manifest through the lives of people. I wonder if we have a situation in life where the subtle awakening of heart energy is so obscure that it appears to be naturally there to those who easily manifest it and naturally missing to those who act as though it doesn't matter and who therefore don't even try to manifest it? Or even wish they could!

This conundrum reminds me of the experience of going deaf, when you don't notice what sounds you've been missing until you get a hearing aid. The shock of hearing birds singing again is often startling to someone who has become deaf.

Another shock is after the experience of going slowly blind with a developing cataract and then having cataract surgery that brings the world into focus or colors into life. "I never knew I was seeing all colors with a yellow tint!" "I didn't really notice before that distant objects had been getting so fuzzy."

We don't have an internal radar that says to us, "Hey, there's something out there you're not hearing; hey, there's something out there you're not seeing!" "Hey, love is all around you; why don't you notice it?" "Hey, the world needs much more love right now from you; do you have a little to spare?"

When people grow to adulthood missing most of the energy of their heart center, perhaps they are not aware that

25

something vital is absent. "Vital" is the word I choose here because there are all kinds of life-guidance decisions, spiritual awareness insights and emotional maturity characteristics that are compromised when you wander the planet with insufficiently developed heart energy. The number of people who feel "lost" testifies to how vital it is. The state of the world testifies to its limited availability.

Unfortunately, in my experience heart energy is not just either missing or present. There seems to be a continuum that goes from an extreme of extravagant heart emotionalism or narcissism on one end to anger, violence, hatred or psychopathic absence at the other. There is no "built-in rheostat" that allows us to easily move along this continuum and select the setting that works just right for each of us in every moment. And perhaps, if given that rheostat, we wouldn't know where to set it anyway!

What this suggests, however, is the importance of knowing enough about your heart energy so that you can regulate your life in relationship to how love is being called from you by the situations in which you find yourself. So knowing yourself well enough to make this possible would seem worth your while. Right?

The best explanation I know for what heart energy is all about is that we have seven energy centers in the human body of which many of us aren't explicitly aware. Three of these are closely connected to the manifestation of heart energy: Head, heart and gut are the terms most frequently used to refer to these centers.

Head usually refers to the brain's intellectual capacity, typically thought of as located above the neck. We spend most of our early years studying, thereby developing this intellectual capacity. Some of us think that the head is the only important aspect there is to us; that the rest of the body is just for keeping the head alive and functional. But the head alone is a "lost child."

Unless we grow up in an environment that immerses us in music or the arts for extensive periods, we typically spend the first two or three decades of our lives in schools focused on intellectual activity. Many males are traditionally overdeveloped from the neck up. (Females have generally been more acclimated to and comfortable in their emotional heart center, although generalizations relating to a sexual distinction in this regard may be becoming obsolete due to increasing awareness and acceptance of feminine energy.)

However, it is not easy for rigorous students to open and live in their heart center, since the demand for academic performance too often channels them into their heads. The more focused the academic, the more likely he or she is to be absent from influences of the heart.

Gut refers to our instinctual center, located in the belly. This center is a major trigger of physical energy, as it manifests in instructions to either fight and engage, or run away to fight another day. This instinctual urge may recognize an emotion, such as fear or the memory of an experience, and adjust as it manifests into action.

Your gut may be the first to react to a situation better left to your heart. It may take some unwelcome episodes to allow this to dawn in your consciousness. Gut energy too often overrules the heart center, especially when the heart is insufficiently open or aware.

Heart refers not to your physical heart but to a place in the center of your chest just above the base of your breastbone. Energetically, the heart center is where emotional intensity can build and where most of your emotions physically manifest. It is also the only center that accesses your spiritual capacity and your soul's wisdom, two good reasons to pay attention to it!

The path to healing and to God is through the heart, not through the intellect. Studying about God is very different from being in God. The heart center is also where the leadership of your own life is felt and available. When it comes to making decisions that result in happiness, the heart center is the wisest place to be, which is why in our culture so many feel lost - - they are too uncomfortable being peaceful long enough to intuit the answers that mean the difference between happiness and misery.

So, if your answer to violence is to love, then knowing love and being able to come from a loving place in your heart makes sense. Merely acknowledging the word "love" as significant misses the point. If you can intellectually define love, then you are on the wrong track. Only if you can FEEL love is the word now alive within you, and when it is alive within you, you can no longer define it because it is experienced in a place that defies definition. (Defining is an exercise of the intellect, not of the heart!)

Many males live in their intellect and gut centers, allowing their hearts to hide out. Many females live in their gut and heart centers, allowing their intellects to hide out. People living with their three centers balanced and functional may be in the minority.

Being in your heart is a very different place from being in your head. If God is love and love is living in your heart, then violence is impossible. But if love is really alive in your heart and you have learned how to transform your life into one of coming from love, then violence is anathema. This is what Gandhi meant when he said: "Be the change you want to see in the world."

Being in your heart is easy in the absence of fear and anxiety. When the heart is intimidated by these forces, it often takes courage to resist the call of the gut to fight, and instead pursue the way of peace.

The Dalai Lama said, "True peace with ourselves and the world around us can only be achieved through the development of mental peace." What he is saying is that internal peace in everyone, one at a time, is necessary for world peace. You cannot learn what peace is by understanding and agreeing with the definition of peace. You have to be at peace, living your life from there in order to be peace.

Your heart center can be closed, partway open, totally open, or anywhere in between. The more open the heart center, the more capacity you have to be loving. To love is a choice, but to manifest love requires the heart center to be open. The pertinent question then becomes: How do I open my heart center so that I can choose to love?

The bottom line is that **you can only love another to the degree you love yourself**. This is a truth that should be of vital concern to Christianity and other major religions. My training to become a therapist required me to recognize this truth. I often felt thankful for clients who brought up personal issues that pushed my buttons and forced me to deal with what was in me that needed to be healed before I could be helpful to them. My clients thereby enabled my own healing process.

In other words, the sacred seeing of your own self may enable you to see more clearly how you are functionally immersed in the life of another, how the relevant intimacy is called forth that can unite your being with another being in a mutually healing relationship.

STEP 4: Opening the Heart

The first requirement for opening your heart center is to choose to do it. This may occur without a conscious decision if you feel attracted to it. But for those who have unconsciously chosen to avoid that commitment, it takes a change in focus.

Typically in my experience, females seem naturally more empathetic than males and find an open heart to be socially and culturally easy. They often slide into open-heart facility without being consciously aware of doing so. However, if they have been abused, physically, emotionally or spiritually, their hearts may be closed if that abuse has made them feel fearful, anxious or alone. Feeling vulnerable and fearful may close your heart. Opening it again may take some internal work in a safe place in order to reach an internal state that accepts the past and has sufficient self-knowledge to resist closing down in the presence of apparent adversity.

Males, on the other hand, have very often been culturally indoctrinated not to show emotions except for aggressiveness; so we find that they can show up in life with mostly-closed hearts. One of the values of teenage romantic experiences for males is that they can learn to ameliorate cultural expectations that would otherwise keep their hearts closed. Nevertheless, even though they may find it advantageous to cautiously open their hearts in romantic encounters, expectations of others to the contrary may make this tentative rather than permanent. Defying one's culture can be intimidating!

For example, military duty or sports, calling for aggressive action may not encourage exposure of heart energy except as it is called out for the performance of duties or assignments. The heart energy of tenderness, for example, may not be rewarded very highly, if at all. "Girly-men" and "sissies" are labels "real men" often have to fight in order to "make it" in front of their peers. On the other hand, "team spirit," brotherhood or "*Semper Fi*" may open heart energy in a comfortable but limited way.

For those males influenced by culture or abuse, the choice to open their hearts may be a serious challenge, especially at a younger age. As men mature and discover they are missing something in their approach to living, very often by the age of thirty-five, there is an emotional experience or trauma that calls for consciously opening their heart.

In my workshops, I use a physical metaphor to help people understand what opening the heart is all about. I bring in an empty glass bowl eight inches in diameter by about five inches in height. I refer to this empty container as the open heart at birth, somewhat like a virgin soul. Then I begin to fill it with marbles, explaining with each new marble that this is "being forced through the birth canal," "feeling forceps grasp you at delivery," "being held upside down and slapped," "experiencing rejection at the nipple," "being circumcised," "being told to shut up," "being

32

spanked," etc. We all experience, as we get older, rejection, hurt, and all of life's "slings and arrows" until we may come to the point of exasperation when "we can't take it anymore." (Our bowl of marbles can become full to overflowing with unprocessed feelings from trauma or abuse.)

The number of suicides among veterans of war attests to the widespread unhealed trauma resulting from national policies that place our children in harm's way. Facing the truth of killing others, especially at close range, doesn't square with the value of love and kindness our children are typically expecting to find in their world. Killing is alarmingly dysfunctional, if not anathema, in the world of sacred seeing. When soldiers are forced to kill, the sacred is eviscerated from their beings. I wonder if this is part of the answer to why it is so difficult for returning vets to find love in relationships.

The "romance" of warfare and the patriotic zeal dreamed of are the first casualties of the face-to-face requirement to kill or be killed. Computer games may lose significance after this kind of trauma, which can grip and traumatize the unprepared heart. The soldier returns home to find out that nobody understands. In fact, he or she doesn't even understand. Nobody else's heart can empathize with such an experience except for those of trained therapists who know what happens to wounded hearts. Even then, without sacred seeing, the blossoming therapist is handicapped in efforts to salve such sacred wounds.

33

Coming back to the marbles, as soon as people in the workshop begin to relate to their own experiences, I dump the remaining marbles into this container until it is all filled up. This I call the closed heart because it is so full of embodied negative experiences that have not had a chance to be released, there is no room for the positive heart energy of love or the capacity for spiritual wisdom to be accessible.

What is necessary to heal this over-laden heart is to release the energy in your body that is tied up with each of your marbles. The healing task is to love each marble by focusing on it, paying attention to it and nursing it so that the embodied negative energy dissipates. Then that marble can be set-aside in the "been-there-done-that" recording of your spiritual journey.

One of the disciplines of this heart therapy is to keep a journal of your process so that you can invest in your own witnessing of what you need to go through in order to clean out and make holy your own bowl of marbles.

What I did on my spiritual journey was to use my word processor to type my negative energy onto a private disc. Often I would type with my eyes closed in a kind of meditative style, recording whatever came into my head until the energy feeling in my body around the issue (marble) was no longer present. I would take whatever time was needed to completely exhaust the feelings that were attached to the issue (marble).

So what does it take to transform your life so that you can be peace? It basically means going through an extensive process of accepting who you really are, cleaning out most of the negative energy of emotional garbage you have collected over your lifetime as marbles, and arriving in a spiritual emptiness of pure love. Then you can feel peaceful and live in sacred peace. There is no other way.

Purifying your heart is an essential step on the spiritual journey. Self-acceptance is your personal garbage-disposal unit. But to use it you need to face up to all the "slings and arrows of outrageous fortune," and forgive yourself for all your training shortcomings, for your life up to this moment has been mere training for today and tomorrow.

One method helpful in this process of purification, when working with one of your marbles, is to locate where in your physical body the energy of that marble seems to reside. By touching yourself in that spot as you work with its energy you will find it easier to focus on it.

It is also important to be aware of the power of your own curiosity as you work with your marble of the moment. You can talk to your spot and ask it questions. Assume that it can answer you; you just need to be patient with it, listening within your body for the intuitive response and then trusting that response so that you can ask the next question. Curiosity, patience and trust are critically important as you work with yourself.

This takes personal courage and a willingness to take total responsibility for everything in your life, regardless of whether it happened *to* you. Your spiritual goal in life is to become who you really are, and who you really are is who you discover yourself to be in the process of this purification.

Who you really are is what's left after the purification process. Purifying removes negative energy from your emotional and physical body. As you do this, you begin to sense what the positive aspects of your life have been all about. When you add up the positives, you come to accept yourself as you really are. As the negative energy dissipates, the power of your essence becomes internally visible and inherent.

Your natural leadership and creativity are the by-products of the journey of awakening to your "self." Leadership is not something that can be taught; it is what naturally arises from doing this work on your self. Knowing who you are and what you stand for provide the wherewithal for manifesting natural leadership and creativity.

That is when you understand your true power that arises from within during purification; it is the power that enlivens you from within like an erupting volcano and empowers your life in the world. It is like a flower erupting from within its seed to become who you are.

So how does this happen?

STEP 5: Your Soul Guides Your Process

The mystery of the universe deepens when you begin seriously to work on your self. Your soul knows at all times what you need to heal. We heal from the inside out. All of our experience with wounds and cuts is that scar tissue forms over the trauma and the healing begins automatically from deep within, like a fire sprinkler that goes off when the heat gets too high.

The same is true with psychological and spiritual wounding: Your soul knows what is most important to bring up in the moment. All we need to do is to recognize it, spend the appropriate time with it and process it until it is complete, until there is no longer any energy around it. When we're done, our soul, in its own time, brings up the next thing we need to pay attention to! It's wonderful! Like an automatic candy dispenser that always has the next candy bar spring-loaded and available for the taking.

So there is no planning needed in this process; the only thing necessary is to stay open and aware for the next issue to show up and then to pay attention to it until its energy dissipates. What this means is that we all need to spend time in silence, meditating on what is in our heart right now. And this calls for giving your self the gifts of serious attention and curiosity. This is what playing marbles is all about!

Of course, this isn't about candy, either! Our soul chooses what we need to work on, and much of that is not sweet or easily digestible. To deal with what comes up often takes courage and intestinal fortitude. You may need to work with a therapist who can help you focus on it and get into it safely. Curiosity, exploration, perseverance and patience are your tools during this time.

Don't worry if you don't "get it" right away. Patience with your self is key. Things take time. Just keep coming back to focus on what is unresolved. In time, your heart will come to know the answers you need.

Life crisis often begins around the age of thirty-five to forty. By then we have sufficient life experience to understand that our dreams for living life may not be a realistic expression of what our soul requires. The universe has a way of finding situations that challenge us to find the path the soul would have us be on. If we ignore this calling, we pay a price.

I had a client whose father insisted he go into business management. He gave it a good try for much too long but discovered that some of the situations in which he found himself made him physically ill. His values were just not compatible with what the business called him to do. He became ill because he was trying to do what his father wanted without understanding that the psychosomatic penalty for this dishonoring of his own soul was to become physically sick. His soul wanted him to be who he really was, not who his father wanted him to be.

This finally got resolved when his father died, releasing him from his self-made, dead-end trap. His desire to be of service to others just couldn't be fulfilled in the business settings his father chose for him. It took a long time for him to understand that emotionally and spiritually he could not do what his father wanted, even though he could physically show up and go through the motions.

So now you see that focusing on each marble in turn as it appears is how you enable your soul to facilitate the opening of your heart. But what do you have to do to make this happen?

STEP 6: Facing the Darkness Within Until You Find the Light at the End of the Tunnel.

This is not an easy path. But it is essential to holistic and spiritual living. There is a Sufi story of Rasmussen[8], who is discovered by a priest one night searching in the dirt near a lamppost. Naturally curious, the priest inquires what the man is doing. "I'm searching for my lost keys," the man says. Motivated by compassion, the priest joins in the search. After some time in this shared effort, the priest points out, "We're not getting anywhere! Where, more precisely, do you think you lost those keys?" Rasmussen, without hesitation, points and says, "Over there in the darkness somewhere," and keeps on with the search in the dirt within the lamp's illumination. The priest, now perplexed, inquires, "But why are we searching here?" "Because," says Rasmussen, "the light is brighter here!"

Like Rasmussen, searching for the keys to life under a lamppost "because the light's brighter here," we all must eventually realize that the important keys are down the road, in the darkness of our internal being.

This is about slowing down your pace of living and taking time to be in silence, searching in the darkness of your internal being for the keys to your life. Or, I should say, marbles! But it is not so much searching, as allowing

---

8. Rasmussen is the "fool" of Islam's Sufis. He is used to impart spiritual lessons.

time for your soul to make manifest the particular marble that needs attention right now. There is nothing strenuous about this process; it calls for relaxing and accepting rather than energizing and judging. It calls for living in silence for periods of time with a new form of insight.

Recently, a participant in one of my groups remarked that he had been studying and preaching all his life, but this was the first time he realized how little time he had spent in silence. His comment implied that he was finding value effortlessly in the process of being silent and allowing his marbles to arise into conscious attention.

This process is often referred to as one kind of meditation. The process of relaxing and going within into the darkness, is to focus attention on what comes up into consciousness and treating that as holy, as worthy of veneration.

Many meditation styles attempt to have you bypass "monkey-mind" by using a mantra or breath work to remove what is coming up into consciousness from conscious attention. Assuming you are seriously engaged and focused on cleaning up your dysfunctional marbles to begin with, this meditation I suggest calls you to focus on and pay attention to what arises rather than trying to escape from it. It calls you to notice what you are paying attention to—and what you are not paying attention to—that is otherwise calling itself to your consciousness.

There are many things I could say about this kind of meditation, but I want to leave you with the impression that there are not a lot of rules you need to follow. Therefore, I hesitate to say too much and by so doing limit the freedom you have to follow your soul's guidance.

The most important consideration is to commit to spending time seeking your marbles in the silence of meditation. I typically meditate for twenty to thirty minutes per day. I find the best time to do this is early in the morning after exercise and before breakfast. By following this schedule, it can become routine. You will be awake, conscious and ready to work into this relaxation process. Not having eaten, your blood flow will not be diverted from your brain to your digestive track.

I feel that much instruction about doing meditation correctly is dysfunctional guidance for the process that I am calling you to do. The requirements are to be in silence and pay attention in mindfulness. Nothing else is necessary. Using a mantra and/or toning "ummmmm" may be unnecessary diversions from the internal silence that will bring you to peace. You may eventually get to the point where your soul feels at peace and surrounded by love using these other methods, but just being in silence does the job for me.

The more you engage in daily silent meditation, the more your level of stress will diminish. You will notice that you seem more calm and serene, and that the problems that show up in daily life are less disturbing and more easily handled.

It is important during the process of meditation, when something with emotional energy arises, to locate where in your body from which the energy seems to come. Then it is helpful, in order to understand this energy, to take your focus there and stay with it until it gives you a message of some kind. Often it may soften. You may feel it dissipate, or you may envision a symbol of some kind that is a message from your soul to pay attention to. Your heart is very creative in this regard!

Pay attention! If a symbol comes up, ask it why it is there and what it's message is. Engage yourself in your inner life and seek explanations for the mysterious.

This is particularly important with the emotion of anger. Because anger is so difficult to deal with under any circumstances, a useful practice is to use some props to feel it deeply enough to cause it to dissipate. You might squeeze a rubber ball, smash a tennis ball with an overhead serve, or beat a hanging rug or a pile of cushions with a tennis racket or baseball bat. While dissipating this energy, it is important to keep the feeling of anger in focus. If it is being carried in your gut, for example, then be aware of it in your gut as you strike the object. Project power that relates to the intensity of your feeling. Feel the energy of anger releasing onto the object, the tennis ball, the rug, or the cushions.

It is important to take whatever comes up in meditation that disturbs you and follow it through to release and dissipation. Most emotions can be handled in the silence, but occasionally an emotion like anger can call for a more vigorous response so that you can touch it viscerally in the process.

There is one caveat I need to mention here. If you are a victim of violence and have symptoms of PTSD that make it especially difficult to do this work, I suggest you find a therapist to help you. You may also find it relevant to consult Serene Jones' book *Trauma + Grace.*

Finally, you may come to understand that the spiritual journey you're on is what you're doing right now, wherever you are. If you are aware of all that is going on in your life and how you are being called to come out of hiding, then the journey becomes very exciting. Writing this up as you do it is a treasured resource. You won't believe where you've been until you look back and see where you were. I know!

STEP 7: Playing with Your Holy Marbles

It seems important now to look at some examples of marbles that I have been privileged to witness as I've worked with clients over the years. The intention here is to help you to envision what working with your marbles is all about.

One client with whom I worked was a professional therapist who couldn't understand why she wasn't happy with her life. She was unmarried and lonely while her professional practice was doing OK. She had spent years worrying about her loneliness and had tried going out on dates but without success. She came to me because I was focused on using heart energy in the service of love.

As we worked with her "marble," I asked her in one session why she had chosen to become a psychiatric therapist. As she explained her motivation, I got an intuitive "hit" that she really was using her role as a professional to distance herself from people, that she was frightened of intimacy. She worked from behind a desk to keep physical distance from her clients As we probed further, she realized that she was a mature woman who had no reason to be fearful, that this fear had arisen in response to violation and abuse of her space earlier in life. She had unconsciously projected this violation into her choice of vocation and, in spite of her professional training, had never before faced so explicitly this fear of intimacy.

The result of our work was to enable her to feel a deep freedom about who she was and what she might be able to do with her life. Opportunities were opening up for her that involved a complete change in occupation, which meant leaping into love with her new, free self. Her joy was palpable as she loosened into her new life. As part of her celebration of this new life, she sent me a card depicting Dorothy's red shoes from *The Wizard of Oz*, and thanking me for helping her "return to her home (in Kansas.)"

Another client was a professional businessman who had always worked as an employee. He wanted to start his own company but something was holding him back. As we talked, it became apparent that he had moved around quite a bit during his career, but each time he quit or was fired, he avoided taking responsibility for failing on the job, instead placing the blame elsewhere. Eventually, he admitted that he couldn't handle failure. (He couldn't even say the word without hesitation!)

He had excellent credentials and a significant background in his chosen business. He was full of energy and excited about making the change, but he just couldn't bring himself to cut the cord of "being employed." He was looking at a major fear in his life without realizing what was happening. It was as though there would be nobody else to blame except for himself if he failed.

To him, this felt like jumping off a cliff without a lifeline. In reality, it was only a step off into a new direction, but that isn't how it felt. He finally faced his fear

47

and agreed that the only option was to do it.[9] Which he did! Once committed, the step "into the unknown" was easy. He never looked back, feeling free and energized, at last in charge of his own life and free to really BE. The feeling was of having a large weight lifted off his back, or like stepping through an opaque membrane into a beautiful landscape of possibility. There was a palpable feeling of transformation! His fear dissolved in action.

Another client was a psychiatric charge nurse who worked in a highly stressful job in a hospital setting and was on Prozac, an anti-depressant drug that she hated but felt dependent upon. She asked me to help release her from the psychological grip of the drug. The "marble" was dealing with the job stress in a different way so as to allow a more "alive" response to living her life.

What she noticed was that she felt so angry that she couldn't relax into what she used to love to do: painting and playing music. It was like the drug seemed to mask her sense of creative presence and aliveness. As we worked with the anger, she discovered that she was living a life at work that was so efficient and busy that when she arrived home after work she had no energy or motivation left to be who she felt herself to really be. Her sense of being felt emasculated. It was like there was no room in her life for her to be who she was.

---

[9] Goethe, the philosopher and writer, said: "Whatever you can do or dream you can, begin it; boldness has genius, power and magic in it."

As we probed this aspect of her "marble," she realized she had to release her anger and change her life's work. She used her drawing skills to bring in two portraits of herself: one the stiff, busy, serious, focused nurse automaton who was stressed out by work; the other an angel who lived and floated on gossamer wings in a world of art and music. It was like her work persona used up so much of her life's energy that her angel was starving, all shriveled up in a corner of her memory of a different way of being that she remembered and longed for.

In a memorable scene one day in my office, she took off her nurse's cap, pulled out her hair clips and pins and let her hair down around her shoulders. She was so determined to transform herself that she dramatically demonstrated the change she felt she wanted, flipping her unconstrained hair around in a new sense of freedom.

She decided she really wanted to be the soft, creative angel, not the busy, negative nurse. Once she assimilated the reality of what this meant to her, she began to make changes in her life that soon meant retiring from her nursing career, moving with her husband to a new area, and devoting herself to drawing out, resurrecting and becoming the angel she truly was. The need for Prozac had vanished like a bad dream.

The above three examples should give you a sense of what "marbles" are all about. They are all holy in the sense that resolving them teaches you about your self and makes your soul feel more whole. If playing with your

49

marbles is too intimidating, get help from a therapist. Once you've made some progress and stepped out into aspects of your new self, you may find that you can handle what comes up in a daily meditation You can do this, but it takes patience and perseverance.

STEP 8: So What Is Your Soul Doing Here Anyway?

I have been making references to your soul, as though you know exactly what I mean. You really do! But you may not be willing to recognize it.

There is a body of literature that posits the existence of a soul in each one of us, including the notion that we live many lifetimes in different milieu. The general theory is that we are not who we think we are, but instead are spiritual entities on a journey whose purpose is to live what we have come to call "life," and thereby experience incarnation so that we learn who we really are, spiritually.

This suggests that we may be here to learn spiritual lessons and that life on earth is a kind of cosmic school of the spirit. This is not universally accepted, but it seems to be a useful handle on what is really going on.

Whether you choose to believe this or not, it is a useful framework on which to hang your self-portrait. It gives you a point of view that enables you to empower yourself with self-assurance, once you have a sense of the power within and "know" where you fit in the "scheme of things."

Therefore, useful questions to ask in meditation include: Who am I, really? Why am I really here in this world at this time, a product of this family of man? What am I called by my soul to do in this life? What will complete my life's journey, assuming everything up until this moment has been training for my future? If I assume I chose everything in my life for a purpose, what would that purpose be—e.g., why did I choose my mother, father, siblings, place of birth, where I grew up, the schooling I mastered, etc.?

You may find that other people in your world object to your being the person you really are. You have to decide what is most important to you. My experience is that you pay a huge price for sacrificing yourself on the altar of someone else's prescription for you. Your heart is all you really have in life. Honor it! The alternative is to live heart-broken. As an obvious oxymoron, that possibility is not viable once you recognize it as such.

STEP 9: Love Lives in Your Heart

When you begin to ask questions like this and immerse yourself in exposing your marbles to "the light," you may begin to notice that you are becoming lighter, like the burdens you've been carrying in your backpack of worries suddenly seems smaller and less weighty. Isn't this an interesting juxtaposition of words? Exposure to the light makes the marbles lighter! And we thought all this time that we were in the darkness of our inner being. What a shock to discover we were deluded into thinking our inner being was so reprehensible and unforgiving!

Are we really this beautiful?

When we come to know who we really are, then we can't avoid comprehending that we are a facet of love, of God's energy. To discover that we are not our work in life, that we are not the names that people call us, that we are really a work of marvelous beauty and holiness—this is to discover our essence, who we really are. Being immersed in the mystery of our own lives is to marvel at the wonder of it all, of everyone around us, of the planet's people.

And so we come to sense a glimpse of the love that got us to where we are. This sense can only deepen as we dig around among our personal marbles, coming to deeply appreciate them for what they have taught us. What you thought were your worst experiences and characteristics turn out to be precious facets of the jewel that is you, sparkling in the sunlight. It turns out that your experiences have framed you in perfection.

Isn't this amazing?

Now do you see why learning to love is so important and so necessary?

What would the world be like if everyone embarked on and enjoyed this journey?

The truth is that you are a precious facet of God's jewelry, sparkling in the light of your purpose here on the planet. When you come to appreciate this truth, then life becomes joy and your freely chosen work becomes a blessing.

Can you imagine that this is how Jesus felt after his "forty days and forty nights in the wilderness?" Assuming that the number, forty, is metaphoric, could this be a reference to Jesus dealing with his own marbles on his spiritual journey that may have taken years of reflection and meditation and, just as you are doing, discovering the love that lived in his heart?

STEP 10: What Does It Feel Like to Be in This Place on Your Journey?

If this doesn't feel like peace, then you still may have inner work to do! My experience of this process is suddenly discovering the brilliance of loving energy and an epiphany of the spirit that catapulted me into a place of peace.

It may surprise you to know that I have a master's degree in business administration on top of military training as an officer in the United States Air Force, on top of an engineering undergraduate degree with its technical discipline, all followed by many years of management experience. I was taught to plan and control everything. I learned how to solve problems and get things done, and I became very good at accomplishment. It took a lot of hard work to become competent at enough things that I could meet the challenges I had to face.

With my heart opening in meditation, I learned to "let go, let God." I learned the way in which patience allows "the universe" to guide me, unfolding opportunities as time allows. Synchronicity became real for me. Part of my opening was learning to trust my intuitive signals and realize they came through the grace of God.

Writing this book was unplanned; it's just happening. I feel like I'm being led to find the next word. I have no idea what is coming next! I feel immersed in it as in a pool of water without goggles—everything is a blur except the next word, sentence or idea.

And the most important part of this is the peace I feel as I swim in the pool. It is like the universe is supporting my floating immersion. What a contrast to the way I was taught! Instead of applying myself with gritted teeth to an energetic struggle, I relax and let it come. I go with "the flow," at peace in a wider world that is anything but peaceful. For me, the joy is that I can let go of all that and be in the moment, immersed in this process of peaceful creativity. I can leave in the next moment and return to my focus when my spirit moves me.

I have learned to be very patient with the universe. It manifests what I think I want in its own way, in its own time. I merely put out what I want as it occurs to me, sometimes taking opportunity as it comes. I know what I want to manifest and consciously seek it but patiently await its coming. Most often, it just happens.

What I seek (my focused intention) is an overall sense of loving the world. How this is supposed to happen is up to the universe. Instead of making it happen, I pause in the parenthesis (...) between is and becoming, full of the potential of love, and let God do the work.

And the weird thing about this is that I am writing now just prior to an evening workshop at my church on the **Power of Love in Deepening Faith.**

So, we are at the end of the Ten Steps, but you may have only begun your internal process. By themselves, these steps are not difficult, but they call you to make inquiries about areas of your life to which you may never have given serious thought. So let's take a look back at where we've been.

Why Is Love So Important?

To answer this question is to revisit the world out there and notice what's going on. Then ask the question: If love were the dominant energy in this situation, what would be happening that is different from what is happening?

Child abuse; abuse of women; Wall Street tycoons ripping the world apart for money; war; rape; abuse of drugs like opium and OxyContin, to name only two; bombing innocent civilians ("collateral damage"); refugees left homeless and without employment by war; destruction of homes and places of work in wartime bombing; suicides by returning veterans and others; abuse of employees and weaker people by those in positions of authority; poisoning by agribusiness in the name of greed; abuse of animals; stripping the sea of fish; poisoning water with chemicals; poisoning the air with mercury and other pollutants; politicians who lie; governments run by and for big business oligopolies; the neglect of justice almost everywhere in the world; unemployment; poverty; and crime (white collar and otherwise).

The list could go on for many pages; the above just scratches the surface. If there was any love at all in the vicinity of these monstrosities, would that make a difference?

When you consider that all of the monstrosities involve people who implement them, what if those people had a change of heart? Or even thought about making a difference of a courageous new sort: one that invoked the energy of love? Wouldn't it be fantastic if they had sufficient self-empowered confidence to take a stand for what is right?

Wouldn't it be wonderful to have a "come-to-love" moment in our world? I wonder if there are some preachers out there in need of a new focus? Hmmmmmmmmm!

The Way to Peace

Have you ever wished for peace? Is peace even on your radar screen? What would the world at peace look and feel like? Can you imagine peace?

One of the ways to check this out is to be at peace, yourself. This condition is a natural fallout from meditation. If you clean out your marbles sufficiently and allow the negative energy in them to dissipate, you will feel peaceful inside. If this condition arises, then envisioning peace in the world is possible, for it will be a natural extension of your sense of peace within.

Is it a reasonable conclusion, then, to suggest that the way to achieve peace in the world is for as many people as possible to meditate and process their way to internal peace?

When love rules our hearts, then peace is possible.

There is no other way to peace. Even if benevolent dictators ruled the world and war was outlawed, the resulting subservience would obviate peace, because peace is a condition of soul freedom within the context of love. True peace (not just the absence of war) requires an eruption of love from within, a suffusion of the energy of love manifested through human beings purposefully immersed in it.

When you feel at peace, even in the midst of chaos, you find that you can be truly present to other people. And if you can tune into them, bringing your own wisdom and heart energy into gear, you are primed to be a mentor for them. Having nothing of your own agenda left to obviate immersed and loving involvement, you are free to be there for them in a way that can be pure and true.

Learning to love is the only path to peace. Peace is the only place from which to come if you aspire to "mentor" love in the world, where it is so badly needed. Amen.

Afterword

Having learned how to love your self, the relevant question then becomes: How do I love others?

Aside from the obvious ways to care for others, to pay attention to them, to assist them where possible, to be in touch with them, to empathize with them, what do you know from your spiritual journey that could be useful? What does your intuitive response to the needs of the world become in the presence of your sacred seeing and internal beauty?

I must leave you with these questions unanswered. To presume to answer them is to impede the journey you need to take, and perhaps the book you need to write. I cannot impose any more on what your creative capacity is capable of producing. I can only leave the questions open for you to play with in your infinite wisdom.

Coming from your revitalized and deepened heart center, and focusing on love, you will naturally love others in a way that feels most loving to them.

Enjoy your immersion in love!

Many blessings!

And now you have experienced sacred seeing in the process of truly seeing who you really are. Imagine this process that we've been through together as the process for BEING in our world together. Imagine your sacred seeing of your world. What a difference! It is all sacred, as are you. The sacred circle is complete. Go in peace!

AUTHOR'S BIOGRAPHY

Rodney J. Ferris was, until retirement, a certified psychotherapist who had worked in manufacturing management and as an organization design consultant to Fortune 500 organizations for about thirty years. His company is **Possibilities Unlimited, Inc.**, where he focused on providing psychological counseling for those seeking direction with career and life changes. He is now writing to capture the essence of his therapeutic practice as a legacy for those attracted to it.

This is his second published book. He is also the author of *HOLY LOVE*, which was locally published and can be found temporarily at www.holylovebook.com.

INDEX